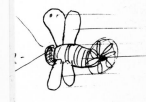

006

D1420922

25415902

Unspun Socks from a Chicken's Laundry

written and illustrated
by

Spike Milligan

and, occasionally, Jane and Laura

M & J Hobbs
in association with
Michael Joseph

Dedication

This book is dedicated to the
unsung genius of Ivor Cutler, who
but for the public's total lack
of appreciation would be a rich man.

First published in Great Britain by M & J Hobbs, 25 Bridge Street,
Walton-on-Thames, Surrey and Michael Joseph Ltd, 44 Bedford Square,
London WC1

1981

ISBN 0 7181 1999 1

Typesetting by D. P. Media Limited, Hitchin, Hertfordshire

Printed in Great Britain by Hollen Street Press, Slough
and bound by Dorstel Press, Harlow

Contents

Foreword

Unspun socks,
from a Chicken's Laundry,
That is the name of this book.
It could have been
Chickens T. Shirts,
or the Monkey Punk Rockers look,
or the knickers of a Pussy cat
or a doggie's woolly vest,
(but!) Unspun socks from a Chicken's laundry
is the title *I* like the best.

Backword

Unspun socks,
from a Chicken's Laundry,
That is the name of this book.
It could have been
Chickens T. Shirts,
or the Monkey Punk Rockers look,
or the knickers of a Pussy cat
or a doggie's woolly vest,
(but!) Unspun socks from a Chicken's laundry
is the title *I* like the best.

Author's Note

These poems are all really inspired by children. Listening to my children talking I noted down the mispronounced, misunderstood words — slips of the tongue, self-invented words, i.e. Bang Clatcher = Gun.

Knowing children's love of vocal exclamation, i.e. Boom! Bang! etc — I've included a few bits with onomatopoeia, and also poems based upon statements and opinions which children have ventured. I am of the opinion that children are not just small *homo sapiens* — they are an entirely different species, with a secret world that only very perceptive adults have any real knowledge of. I have. Lucky me.

Well Bread

If you cast your bread on the waters,
It returns a thousand fold,
So it says in the Bible,
That's what I've been told.

(So) I cast my bread on the waters,
It was spotted by a froggy,
And the bits of bread *he* didn't eat
Just floated back all soggy.

Sheraton Hilton
Hong Kong
Fri. 13 June 1980

The Battle

Aim! said the Captain
Fire! said the King
Shoot! said the General
Boom! Bang! Ping!

Boom! went the Cannon
Bang! went the Gun
Ping! went the Rifle
Battle had begun!

Ouch! said a Prussian
Help! said the Hun
Surrender! said the Englishman
Battle had been won!

**Melbourne
April 1980**

Envoi

Bandage! said the Doctor
Cotton! said the Nurse
Ointment! said the Surgeon
Curse! Curse! Curse!

Hobart
Tasmania
1970

The Glutton

Oh Molly, Molly, Molly
I've eaten too much pie
I've eaten too much custard
I think I'm going to die!

Just one more plate of Jelly
Before I pass away
Another glass of lemonade
And then no more I say!

Perhaps just one banana
And one more lollipop
A little slice of Eccles cake
And then I'll have to stop!

So now one more one more Goodbye!
and one more slice of ham
and now goodbye forever
But first some bread and jam

So now Sadie, goodbye again
But pass the Stilton cheese
And as I slowly pass away
Just one more dinner please.

Ipple-apple Tree

I'm going to plint an apple tree
Not plint, I mean to plant,
You cannot plint an apple tree
You cint, I mean you can't.
I mean you plant
You do not plint
And I mean can't
When I say cint
If you insist and plint a tree
Ipples will grow, not apples you see?

Apple   Ipple

Saudi - Bayswater
Nov 1979

Standing Room Only

'This population explosion,'
Said Peter to St Paul,
'Is really getting far too much,
Just look at that crowd in the hall.
Even here in heaven
There isn't any room,
I think the world could do with less,
Much less fruit in the womb.'
Thus heaven is overcrowded,
the numbers are starting to tell,
So when the next lot knock at the gates,
tell 'em to go to hell.

Slip ware

There's many a slip
Twix cup and lip,
And the sound it makes
Is drip drip drip.

The Elephant

The only animal,
If you please,
That can bend forward
on *all* four knees.
Whoever made him
Did not know
The disproportion
it would show.
Poor Elephant at
his shape must rail,
A nose that's longer
than his tail.

Monkenhurst
July 25, '76

Nothing Poem

There's nothing in the Garden,
and unless I'm losing my sight,
there was nothing again this morning.
It must have been there all night

It's hard to see a nothing
or even where it's been.
This was the longest nothing
that I have ever seen.

I locked all the drink in the cellar
so nothing could get at the gin,
but by skwonkle o'clock in the evening
nothing had got in!

So I bolted the doors and windows
so nothing could escape,
I called for the local policeman
who was armed with a helmet and cape

'I hear there's been a break in
and you might have lost something of worth.
Can you describe the intruder?'
'Yes, he looks like nothing on earth!'

Monkenhurst
26 July 1976

By Gum

Death to the Dentist!
Death to his chair!
Death to his 'this might hurt'!
There! There! There!

Death to his injections!
Death to his nurse!
Death to his amalgam!
Curse! Curse! Curse!

Death to his needle!
Death to his drill!
Death to his 'open wides'!
Kill! Kill! Kill!

Hobart
Tasmania
May 1980

Sean when five said, 'I want to kill the Dentist.'

Bad Report – Good Manners

My daddy said, 'My son, my son,
This school report is bad.'
I said, 'I did my best I did,
My dad my dad my dad.'
'Explain, my son, my son,' he said,
'Why *bottom* of the class?'
'I stood aside, my dad my dad,
To let the others pass.'

Pennies from Heaven

I put 10p in my Piggy Bank
To save for a rainy day.
It rained the *very next morning*!
Three cheers, Hip Hip Hooray!

None today, thank you

The convent rang with explosions all day
As nun after nun was exploded away.
'Something really must be done,'
Said an unexploded nun.
'With such a very fragile exterior
We'll have to armour the Mother Superior.'
So Mother Fabian was covered in steel,
They asked her, 'Mother, how does it feel?'
She whispered as she lit a taper,
'Heavier but much much safer!'
But against the odds, oh! cruel fate!
She exploded that night at ten to eight.
All over the church her bits were scattered,
She was gone and that's what mattered
Said Sister O'Brien, 'Bedad and Begob,
It must have been an inside job.'
Who would want to explode a nun?
It wasn't their idea of fun.
The mystery was solved by Sister Murry:
'Of course, this week we've been eating CURRY!
So peace and quiet returned to the Cloisters,
But no more Curry, Guinness and Oysters.

'Nappy'

'Adieu! mon Emperor Napoleon,'
said brave Marchal Laporte.
'Don't fret my friend,' said Napoleon,
'and call me "Nappy" for short.'
'Why do you cry like a baby?'
someone was heard to say.
'Because,' said the weeping Marchal,
'They have taken my nappy away.'

MacDrown

Urgle urgle urgle
Whatever is that sound?
Urgle urgle urgle!
It's coming from that mound!!

Gurgle gurgle gurgle!
That's urgle with a G!!
The sound that people make I hear
When drowning in the sea!

MacGurgle hic! MacGurgle hic!
Ah, now it's clear to me
A Scotsman drowning in a whisky vat,
A happy death and *free!!*

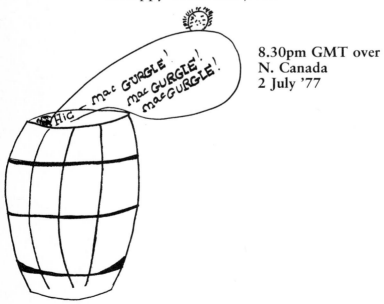

**8.30pm GMT over
N. Canada
2 July '77**

A little hairy monster
Came crawling up to me
He looked so sad and lonely
I asked him up to tea
If only I had known
The fate that wanted me
I'm down inside his stomach
As his favourite recipe

Laura Milligan

↑
Spare part

Hairy monster as envisaged by

James Milligan

25

Winds light to disastrous

As I sipped morning tea,
A gale (force three)
Blew away a slice of toast.
Then a gale (force four)
Blew my wife out the door,
I wonder which I'll miss the most.
She was still alive
When a gale (force five)
Blew her screaming o'er Golders Green,
When a gale six blew
And it took her to
A mosque in the Medanine.
Now I pray to heaven
That a gale (force seven)
Will whisk her farther still,*
Let a gale (force eight)
Land her on the plate
Of a cannibal in Brazil.
As I sat down to dine
A gale (force Nine)
Blew away my chips & Spam
But! a gale (force ten)
Blew them back again,
What a lucky man I am!

Bayswater
1977

* Father Still, a stationery priest

Butterfly

Butterfly, Butterfly
Flitter Flutter Butterfly
Not a bread and Butterfly

Just plain butter, Butterfly.
You ~~total~~ utter Flutterby
You should never ever die
Why tho' are you never spread
On a piece of Butterfly bread?

Perth, WA,
    March, 1980

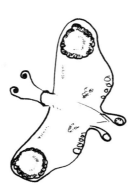

27

Multikertwigo

I saw the Multikertwigo*
Standing on his head,
He was looking at me sideways
And this is what he said:
'Sniddle Iddle Ickle Thwack
Nicki – Nacki – Noo
Biddle – diddle Dicky – Dack
Tickle – tockle – too!
None of this made sense to me,
Maybe it does to you.

* Multikertwigo. A nonsense word my father used
when I was a boy.

28

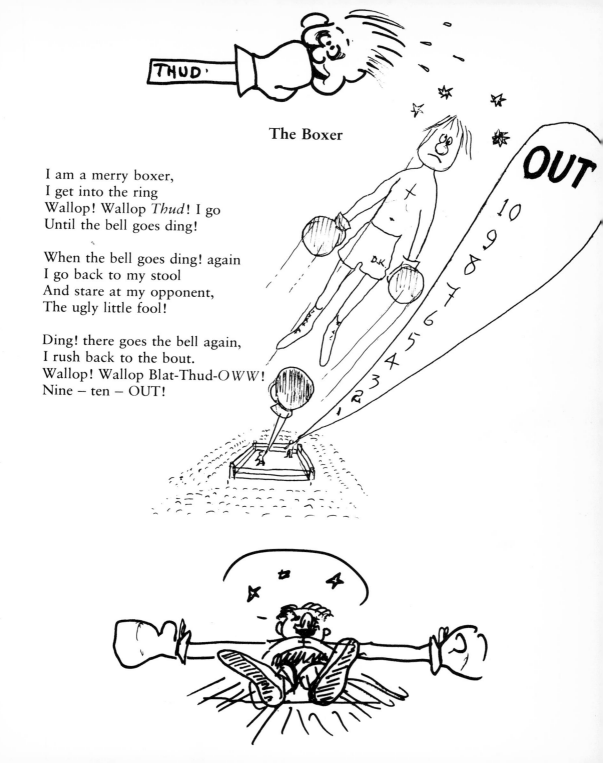

The Boxer

I am a merry boxer,
I get into the ring
Wallop! Wallop *Thud*! I go
Until the bell goes ding!

When the bell goes ding! again
I go back to my stool
And stare at my opponent,
The ugly little fool!

Ding! there goes the bell again,
I rush back to the bout.
Wallop! Wallop Blat-Thud-*OWW*!
Nine – ten – OUT!

Ode to the Queen in Jubilee Year

Sound the trumpet,
Bang the drum,
Shake the Tambourine,
Because this year
Is a Jubilee,
But only for the Quine*

Let us salute her,
Yes let us
Salute her let us yes!
Hiding Marks and Spencers knickers
With Norman Hartnell dress

So Glory Glory
Gloria
Regina Gloriana,
You are the apple**
Of my eye,
Let me be your banana!

*Queen
**Ipple
First published in *Private Eye*
by Private Ingrams

Worm

Little worm – wiggle wiggle,
You make me and my sister giggle.
You live in mud,
You live in wet,
Yet never ever see a vet.
You must be very healthy worm,
Wiggle Wiggle Wiggle Squirm.

The Squirdle

I thought I saw a Squirdle
I think I thought I saw
I think I thunk I thought
I saw a Squirdle by my door

If it was <u>not</u> a Squirdle
I thought I thunk I saw
Then what in heavens was it?
That gave a Squirdle roar?

Perhaps I saw a Pussel-skwonk!
But that would be absurd
Because I think I thunk it was
A Squirdle that I heard

So if I <u>saw</u> a Pussel-skwonk
Yet <u>heard</u> a Squirdle roar
It means I think I thunk I thought
I'd seen what I had saw!

Granddad's Bedtime Story

I'm going to tell a story,
A story I shall tell,
A story of adventure,
of heaven and of hell.
I'll tell it to you children
While you are in your cot,
The time is still quite early,
So I can talk a lot.
And now to tell the story,
One I remember well,
'Twas told me by my father
or was it Auntie Nell?
it might have been my uncle,
I think his name was Fred,
What a lovely man he was,
A pity that he's dead.
He used to tell me stories
of Pirates on the sea,
Which was very strange because
he wasn't fond of me.
He used to have a cat called Tom,
A mangy ginger thing,

and a dog called Dick
with a great big nose
who used to try and sing.
I think they lived near Acton Green
or was it Ponders End?
it was one those – of those I suppose,
now what was the name of his friend?
It wasn't Jim – it wasn't him,
it wasn't Len or Harry.
I *think* it was Bert,
I recall he was hurt
by a man called Looney Larry.
I remember the nurse
Who used to curse
Whenever she dressed his leg.
It was broken, you see,
In two places or three
When he tripped and fell over an egg.
Now I'm going to tell you a story,
Your very flesh will creep.
Once upon a time there was –
Oh dear, they've fallen asleep!

Hong-Bong!

Chinkey Chinkey Chinaman
Living in Hong-Kong,
Give us a tune
On your big brass gong.

Velly Velly Good-ee,
Me beat out a song,
Me in Chinese hit Parade
Bong! Bong! Bong!

Sheraton Hotel
Hong-Kong
Sat. 14 June 1980

Nelly Ninnis

There was a young girl called Nelly
Who had a nylon belly
The skin was so thin
We could all see in
It was full of Custard and Jelly

**By Jane and dad on way back
from Natural History Museum
15 Oct. 1977**

by Jane Milligan

This is a stick-up!

The world seems full of sticky,
It's everywhere I go,
Underneath the table,
And it's moving to and fro.

It follows me to school each day,
It gets into my books,
I swear that I don't put it there
But that's the way it looks.

I've got sticky on my fingers,
Sticky on my clothes,
Sticky inside my pockets,
Sticky up my nose.

My mother keeps on scrubbing
To wash the stick away,
The flannel just gets stuck to me,
My stick is here to stay!

She's hidden all the treacle
And all the sweets she can,
She's locked up all the Syrup
And every pot of Jam.

So *why* am I so sticky
And nicknamed Sticky Sam?
I really-*really* can't believe
How stuck up I am.

**Charlton
Surrey 1979**

He who laughs . . .

I tried to catch an elephant
And then a bull giraffe,
I tried to trap a Hyena
But all he did was laugh.

Ha! Ha! Ha! Ha! Ha! he went,
Then lots of tee-hee-hees,
Ho Ho Ho Ho Ho Chi Min –
Was he Vietnamese?

Auckland, NZ
June 1980

Itchy Koo Land

I wish I were in Itchy Koo land
With a little piece of string.
I'd tie a little bell on it
Ting-a-ling-a-ling!

I wish I were in Itchy Koo land,
A penny in the bank.
I'd draw it out and spend it all
Swank! swank! swank!

I wish I were in Itchy Koo land,
A pot of purple paint.
I'd paint myself from head to foot
And make poor mummy faint!

I wish I were in Itchy Koo land
Where adults never go
And children live for ever
Ying tong iddle i Po!

Silé when aged seven said, 'I wish I was in Itchy Koo
Land.' Thought you'd like to know.

Updated Hubbard

Old mother Hubbard
Went to the cupboard
To get the poor dog a bone.
When she got there,
The cupboard was bare,
So the poor little doggie had Pal.

Gertrude Conk

A rose is a rose is a rose,
and so is a nose is a nose.
Red is the rose,
So is the nose,
And that's how it goes, how it goes, how it goes . . .

A nose, I suppose, I suppose,
grows like a rose, like a rose.
Ah! but the rose
Unlike the *nose*
Doesn't honk! when it blows, when it blows when it blows . . .

A nose, in the throes, in the throes
of a cold in der dose, in der dose.
Hip is a rose
Drip goes the nose,
And that's how it flows, how it flows, how it flows.   .

Hobart
Tasmania
1/2/3 May 1980

Love Conquers

As I watched her walk
Across the Heath,
Black was the colour
Of my true love's teeth.

As I watched him wander
Through the fair,
Bald was the colour
Of my true love's hair.

Hobart
Tasmania
3 May 1980

Tree- kill

1 Chip Chop
Chip Chop
Down comes a tree

2 Chip Chop
Wallop Plop
Help, its fallen on me!.

3 Chip Chop
Chip Chop
Down comes another

4 Chip Chop
Wheee! bop!.
That one fell on mother

5 Chip Chop
Chip Chop
Crash on daddys head!.

6 Chip Chop
Please stop
Or else we'll all be dead!

Music Makers

My Auntie plays the piccolo,
My Uncle plays the flute,
They practise every night at ten
Tweetly tweet *Toot − toot*!

My Granny plays the banjo,
My Granddad plays the drum,
They practise every night at nine
Plankety plank *Bumm − bumm*!!

My sister plays the tuba,
My brother plays guitar,
They practise every night at six
Twankity *Oom − pa − pa*!!!

My mother plays the mouth organ,
My daddy plays oboe,
They practise every night at eight
Pompity-pom suck-blow!!!!

Tim and Jim, Fred and Ned

Hooray Hooray Hooray for Tim,
Hooray for Tim – Hooray for him,
But *no* Hooray for little Jim.
Hooray for Tim – for Tim, *not* Jim.

Hooray Hooray Hooray for Fred,
Hooray for Fred – Hooray, I said.
But no Hooray for little Ned,
Hooray for Fred – for Fred, not Ned!

Tim and Fred get my Hooray,
But not for Jim or Ned I say!

Australia
Feb./March, 1980

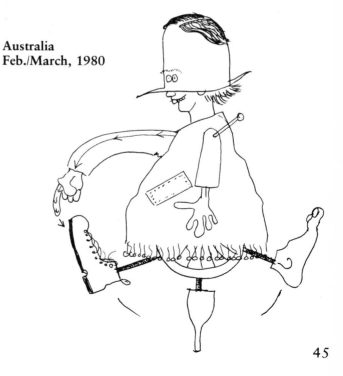

45

Rhymes

Eggs will rhyme with legs
But eggs aren't hairy or fat.
You can boil an egg for breakfast
But legs wouldn't stand for that!

Dog will rhyme with log
But a log isn't man's best friend,
And you can't throw a dog on the fire,
If you did he'd be hard to mend.

Cat will rhyme with Hat
But that my friend is all.
A Hat won't drink a bowl of milk
And you can't hang your Cat in the hall!

Snake will rhyme with Lake
But only the Snake lays eggs.
Otherwise they are both identical,
For neither of them has legs!

Children

What colour is the price
Of those little white mice?
Green and sixpence twice
And they look-taste very nice

Looking in a toyshop window in
Finchley, Silé (about seven) said:
'What colour is the price of
those white mice?'

Airport

Please don't miss Heathrow Airport,
It's only a ten-mile run.
Go there for lunch on a Sunday,
Get in the queue for fun,
Sit in the air-conditioned Restaurant
That keeps all the smell inside.
If you look through the plate-glass windows,
You can see where the flies have died.
Show the kiddies planes taking off
For Paris, Bombay and Rome.
It's only an hour to Paris,
It'll take you four to get home.

Klorstrafibia

Claustrophobia
Means
You don't like things
Around
Under or
Over yer.

The Leetle

Oh the Leetle
Oh the Leetle
Yellow white and blue
Wearing pinkle-ponkle socks
And playing the Didjeridoo

Oh the Leetle
Hands and Feetle
Covered in ginger hairs
Stole a Jelly from the fridge
And rolled it down the stairs!

Then the Leetle
On a Beetle!
Raced right past the Jelly
When he reached the bottom step
It hit him in the Belly!

Oh the Leetle!
Oh the Leetle!
Look what you have done!
Theres Jelly all over the carpet!
Look out! here comes mum!

Don't look in the Biddle-Box,
Little Mary Ann.
The contents of mum's Biddle-Box
Must not be seen by man

Must not be seen by Pussy cats
Or Zebras at the Zoo
And forbidden to all Monkies
Until 1892.

'But 1892 has gone!'
Said Little Mary Ann.
'Oh, so it has,' said Uncle Dick,
'I am a silly Man.'

'So open up the Biddle-Box
And tell us what's inside,
For what you see within that box
'Twas your old mother's pride!'

Slowly then she raised the lid
In that old dusty hall.
Mum's Biddle-Box was empty!
So she had no pride at all!

Quick! bring in all the Pussy cats,
The Zebras from the Zoo
And monkies who've been waiting now
Since eighteen-ninety-two!

Ode to my Mother

If I should die,
Think only this of me,
The swine left owing us
Six pounds eighty p.

Fear-fly

1 If I was a fly
   I don't suppose
   I'd want to land
   On someone's nose.

2 A nose is meant
   To run or drip
   And not used as
   A landing strip.

3 I'd never land
   Upon an ear,
   You never know
   What you might hear.

4 Never land on
   A sailor's belly,
   That's how we lost
   Auntie Nelly.

5 The most dangerous place
   To land I know
   Is either Gatwick
   Or Heathrow.

Poet-tree

I remember a tree
Upon a hill.
If it stood there then,
Does it stand there still?

If it doesn't stand still
And moves about,
Then open the gates
And let it out!

Hobart
Tasmania
29 April 1980

Not-so-hot-dog

My doggie stole a sausage
And ran it down the street,
Discovered it was two-thirds bread
And only one-third meat.

So much bread in sausages
Is against the law.
Even tho' its stolen,
The quality's still poor!

That sausage will not worry,
He knows 'twould be in vain,
For when that doggie's had one bite
He'll run it back again!

And so the English sausage
Was saved from mutilation.
That sausage lived till a hundred and nine
But the dog died of starvation.

If

If I were a Prince
I'd say
Give my socks a rinse!

If I were a Queen
I'd say
Where have you been!

If I were a King
I'd say
Kiss my ring!

If I were a Caesar
I'd say
Arrest that geezer

But as Captain on a Whaler
I say
Hello Sailor!

London

57

Granny boot

Granny in her bed one night
Heard a little squeak!
And then a little
Peck-peck-peck
Like something with a beak
Then something that went Binkle-Bonk
Ickle-tickle-toot
And all of it was coming
From inside Grandmas boot!
Then the boot began to hop
It went into the hall
And then from deep inside the boot
Came a Tarzan call
The sound of roaring lions
The screech of a cockatoo
Today that boot is in a cage
Locked in the London Zoo.

Ah Ah eh
Ah Ah eh
in Tarzan

Grrr etc in
Lion

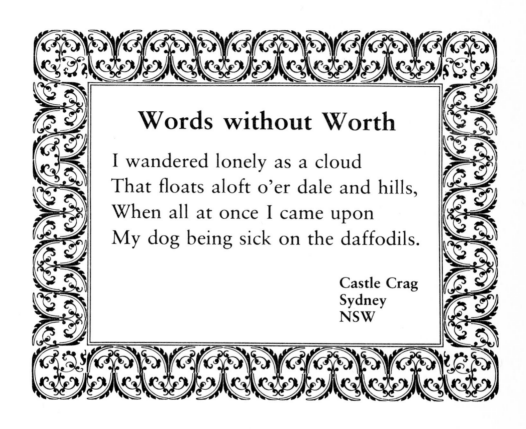

Words without Worth

I wandered lonely as a cloud
That floats aloft o'er dale and hills,
When all at once I came upon
My dog being sick on the daffodils.

Castle Crag
Sydney
NSW

The Ying-tong-iddle-I-po

My Uncle Jim-jim
Had for years
Suffered from
Protruding ears.

Each morning then,
When he got up,
They stuck out like handles
on the F.A. Cup.

He tied them back
With bits of string
But they shot out again
With a noisy – *PING*!

They flapped in the wind
And in the rain,
Filled up with water
Then emptied again.

One morning Jim-jim
Fell out of bed
and got a Po
Stuck on his head.

He gave a Whoop,
A happy shout,
His ears no longer now
Stuck out.

For the rest of his days
He wore that Po,
But now at night
He has nowhere to go.

Castle Crag
Sydney
Feb. 1980

Dedication to Prince Charles
on the occasion of getting the runs
in Australia

You should not eat things
In Alice Springs,
It's those pre-cocktail bits
That give you the squits.*

* Squits

Hamlet

Said Hamlet to Ophelia,
'I'll do a sketch of thee.
What kind of Pencil shall I use,
2B or not 2B?'

Perth, WA
March 1980

Jumbo-Jet

1 I saw a little Elephant
  Standing in my garden.
  I said, 'You don't belong in there!'
  He said, 'I beg your pardon.'

2 I said, 'This place is England,
  What *are* you doing here?'
  He said, 'Ah then, I must be lost,'
  and then, 'Oh dear, Oh dear.'

3 'I should be back in Africa
  On Serengetti's plain.
  Pray, where's the nearest station
  Where I can catch a train?'

4 He took the bus to Finchley
  As far as Mincing Lane,
  Then over the Embankment,
  Where he got lost again.

5 The police they put him in a cell
  But it was far too small,
  So they tied him to a lamp-post
  And he slept against the wall.

6 But as the policeman lay in bed
  By the tinkling light of dawn,
  The lamp-post and the wall were there
  But the Elephant was gone.

7 So if you see an Elephant
  In a Jumbo-Jet,
  You can be sure that Africa,
  Is the place he's trying to get.

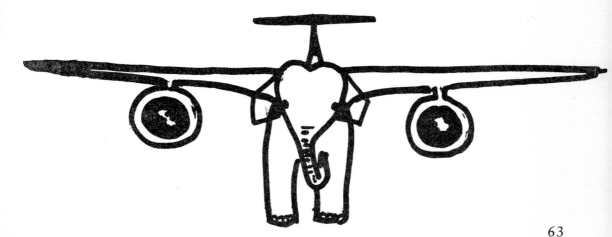

The 'Veggy' Lion

I'm a vegetarian Lion,
I've given up all meat,
I've given up all roaring
All I do is go tweet-tweet.

I never ever sink my claws
Into some animal's skin,
It only lets the blood run out
And lets the germs rush in.

I used to be ferocious,
I even tried to kill!
But the sight of all that blood
made me feel quite ill.

I once attacked an Elephant
I sprang straight at his head.
I woke up three days later
In a Jungle hospital bed.

Now I just eat carrots,
They're easier to kill,
'Cos when I pounce upon them,
They all remain quite still!

Melbourne
April 1980

64

Onamatapia

Onamatapia!
Thud - Wallop - CRASH!
Onamatapia!
Snip - Snap GNASH!
Onamatapia
Whack - thud - BASH!
Onamatapia
Bong - Ting - SPLASH!

Melbourne - Tasmania
April 1980

Kangaroo – Kangaroo!

The kangaroo of Australia
Lives on the burning plain,
He keeps on leaping in the air
'Cos it's hot when he lands again.

Perth, WA
March 1980

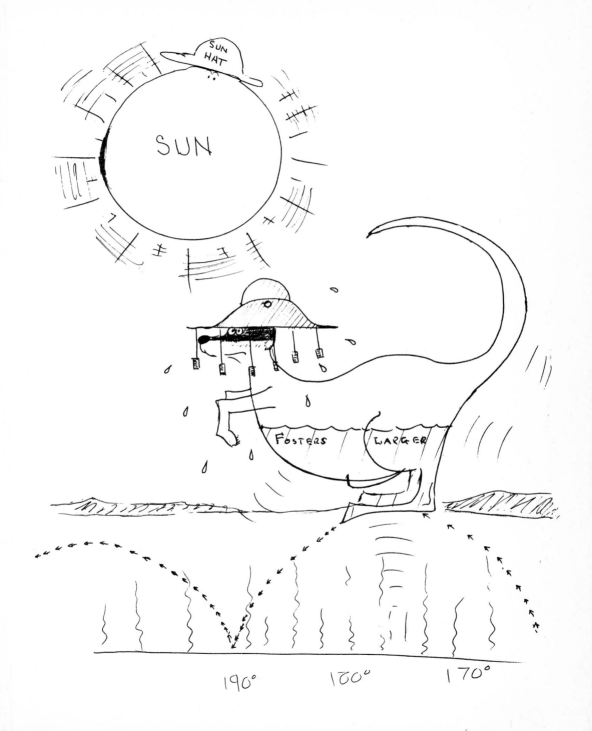

Nice doggie

My neighbours have a barking dog
Bow wow wow wow wow
A little black French Poodle dog
Le Bow Le Bow Le Wow!

There was a time when I loved dogs
Bow wow wow wow wow
I also love good music
Con forte Bow wow wow

So when I listen to Chopin
Dolce Allegro
I also hear a barking dog
Bow wow Fortissimo

Sixteen bars of Chabris
Ompa – Bow wow wow
Then sixteen bars of bark (not *Bach*)
What a bow wow row

And so I'll buy a Tiger
Who'll every night growl ROAR
Then kill and very slowly eat
The Bow wow wow next door.

Started London Jan. '80,
finished Castle Crag,
Sydney, Aust., Feb. 1980

Piffing

Effily Offily
If If If
Niffily Noffily
Piff Piff Piff
I've Piffed at the Baker
I've Piffed at the Beak
Effily Offily
Squeak Squeak Squeak.

1.30am
10 July 1980
In bed
Monkenhurst

Jane invented the word Piffed

How the Dinosaur got here

'Daddy, what's a dinosaur?'
Said my daughter Jane.
'The dinosaur was a giant beast
That will never be seen again.'

'Where did they all come from?'
'Now that I cannot say.'
And at this information
She turned and walked away

She must have thought about it,
For later that afternoon
She said to me, 'I know! I know!
They all came from the moon!'

'If that is true, my daughter,
Would you, pray, please tell
Exactly how they got here.'
She said, 'Of course – they fell!'

Perth, WA
March 1980

My daughter Jane, at the age of ten, said, 'The dinosaurs
came from the moon.' When asked how they got to the
earth, she said, 'They fell.'

Two Funny Men

I know a man
Who's upside down,
And when he goes to bed
His head's not on the pillow, No!
His *feet* are there instead.

I know a man
Who's back to front,
The strangest man *I've* seen.
He can't tell where he's going
But he knows where he has been.

Castle Crag
Sydney, NSW
February 1980

71

Conkerer

I'm going to march on Poland
And then I'll march on France,
Next I'll march on Germany,
I'll lead them such a dance.

I'll smash my way through Russia,
I'll storm all over Spain,
Then I'll go *back* to Poland
And do it all *again*!

I'll conquer all of Asia
From Sweden to the Med.
And then I'll really have to stop,
Mum says it's time for bed.

Hadley Wood
September 1980